The Carinthian Connection

Volume 1

By Howard Koehn

Copyright © 2011 Howard Koehn
All rights reserved.
ISBN: 978-0-578-60996-6

Note from Author

I've always found it curious that ancient Romans, Egyptians, Mayans and Aztecs all once had highly developed advanced civilizations which all had built magnificent cities brimming with magnificent structures and then for some reason, each of their societies collapsed with their structures falling into disarray and decay. Equally curious is post collapse, these civilizations all apparently reverted to a very primitive like existence. ????

My thoughts are - perhaps these ancient societies did not really build these antiquities. These antiquities have the appearance of being remnants of some very large scale ancient commercial enterprise. When I say large scale, I mean spanning the entire planet. My thoughts continue - So, if these antiquities were not built by the ancient Romans, Egyptians, Mayans and Aztecs, then who and why? Whoever they were – they obviously were as technically advanced as we are today.

After extensive study I've concluded - extra terrestrials – and the extra terrestrials had to be the Carinthians.

With that, I then studied the evidence I believe the Carinthians left behind and with this information reconstructed their lifestyle, demeanor, religion, and needs. I have concluded - they lived a lifestyle then, very near the life style we enjoy today, their priorities equally very similar. They loved God, family, life, peace, sports and privilege, in that order. It's my takeaway their level of technological progression exceeded ours today by only 100 years, perhaps only 50. They were indeed very much like us.

All elements of this story have been drawn from some aspect of this evidence. The entirety and specificity of the details that I have written are all pertinent to the full telling of their story.

It appears they colonized Earth on a rigorous scale beginning somewhere close to the year 7988 BC. All indications are they traveled intra-galactic with relative ease and comfort. In chapter 9 I'm going to take you with me and we're going to jump aboard one of their flights and together we will experience how comfortably they made these very frequent voyages.

During their colonization, they brought to Earth advanced levels of technology to assist them in the fulfillment of their quests and desires.

It's obvious they had an insatiable need for raw materials. In 7988 BC, a periodic opportunity to travel to Earth opened for them and they seized on this opportunity to set up mining colonies with a rigorous resolve.

One might feel it's ludicrous to think that a civilization so technically advanced, traveling such distances, would come all the way to Earth with a principal goal of mining. This thought prevails because we tend to think of the consumer goods we use and enjoy all coming from big box stores. The reality is - every cell phone we talk on, every television we watch, every plate we eat from and even this device you're currently reading from, was created with raw materials that someone, somewhere, pumped or dug from this earth. Less than 200 years ago our base raw material needs were largely satisfied with sand, clay, salt, leather, coal and wood. Today our social needs are much more technically sophisticated and consequently so are the raw materials needed to satisfy these societal needs. In this less than 200 years we have critically depleted our known reserves of *rare-earth* raw materials and will need to find new sources soon in order to sustain our social wants.

Most of us perceive the current international exploration of space as a pursuit of knowledge and adventure, but the underlying objective is colonization and mining. So it was with the Carinthians.

The Carinthians opportunistic colonization window lasted for five thousand years and they capitalized on every minute of it. When this window closed they packed up everything they had brought to earth and went home. Evidence and remnants of their existence lie everywhere they frequented here on Earth. This is their story.

PROLOGUE

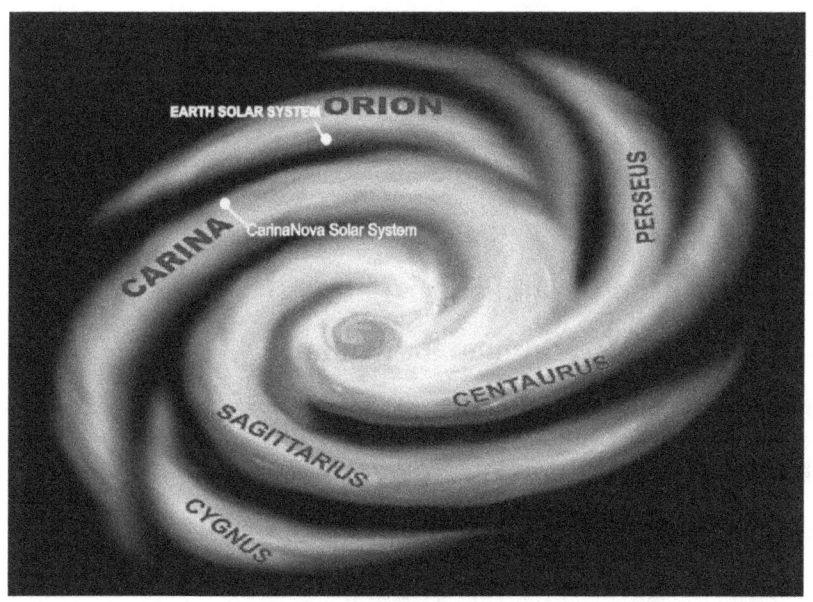

Earth resides in the Milky Way Galaxy. The Milky Way is a spiral galaxy, comprised of six spurs strung from a central hub.

Our Solar System resides in the outer reaches of the Orion spur. The nearest spur to the Orion is the large Carina spur and this is where this story begins.

In the year 7988 BC, Carinthian Missioneers voyaged from the Planet CarinaNova in the mid section of the Carina spur to set up mining colonies on planet Earth.

Table of Contents

Chapter 1 The Carinthians

Chapter 2 The Carinthian Individual

Chapter 3 The Punch Through

Chapter 4 Carinthian Air Power

Chapter 5 Exploration of Earth

Chapter 6 Extermination of Earth

Chapter 7 Colonization Commission

Chapter 8 Special Breeding Program

Chapter 9 Breeding Party Deploys to Earth

Chapter 10 Deployment of the Biologists

Chapter 11 People

Chapter 1

The Carinthians

The Carinthians were an intellectually advanced civilization with a deep history dating thousands of years. Their society consisted of commercially competitive nations of equal power and stature, very prosperous by our current standards.

Religion played a key role in their behavior, but not as an intangible. They fully understood and lived it. The Carinthian's had an unexplainably accessible relationship to their higher deity and were driven by their need to perpetuate His wishes. A strong commitment to a personal relationship with their God formed the fundamental foundation of their law, moral discipline, and behavior.

For many centuries, the nations of CarinaNova had the military power to destroy every living being on their planet through the use of antimatter weapons. These weapons rained lethal gamma rays over very large areas, destroying any living tissue they encountered so that all life over vast stretches could be eliminated in minutes. Unlike nuclear radiation, gamma rays dissipated as soon as the energy was spent, thus no post contamination like that resulting from nuclear radiation. This treacherous capacity to kill made war between nations futile. Any nationally-operated military was too threatening to exist.

With war out of the equation, the Carinthians formed the Joint Arbitration Commission (JACOMM), an international organization comprised of representatives from each nation which arbitrated all international disputes. They founded JACOMM's charter on the principal of insuring the safety and sovereignty of every individual in each nation. The charter also guaranteed to preserve and protect the wealth and power of the individual nations, with JACOMM's role to wholly honor the status quo of all nations.

JACOMM carried out this responsibility with resolve, rigidly enforcing its intent in an expedient and conclusive manner. Carinthians understood and accepted that JACOMM needed to use whatever level of enforcement necessary to insure all parties were treated fairly.

In order to fully discharge their purpose, JACOMM operated an extensive force of men and women, ranging from scientists to soldiers, using a neutral language composed from elements of the various languages used by all nations of CarinaNova. They referred to this language as *English*. Their control extended across all domestic issues and extraterrestrial activity.

In their advanced society, the Carinthians employed the development of matter-antimatter annihilation as the ultimate form of energy. A single gram of antimatter would run a large power plant or space ship for years. Obtained from a large deposit near the galactic hub, antimatter fueled the entire planet of CarinaNova.

The major dilemma for the Carinthians continued to be their lack of natural resources. The age of their civilization, coupled with their massive population, had depleted all the attainable resources from their planet. The Carinthians robust and upscale lifestyle created rampant consumerism resulting in the need to look elsewhere for their raw material needs.

For generations they had maintained mining operations on several moons within their reach, a difficult and costly venture in places with no atmosphere.

Chapter 2

The Carinthian Individual

Unlike the stereotypical description of aliens common on Earth today, the Carinthians were tall, light skinned, athletic, and fit. Their excellent health and physique resulted from evolved genealogy coupled with their lifestyle and diet. They enjoyed a comfortable life free of conflict, rich in leisure, and were wildly enthusiastic about sports and entertainment.

Their principal diet consisted largely of the paltapina, a genetically engineered cross between the avocado and pineapple. The fruit came from a perennial plant over two meters tall. Paltapina plants needed pollination from a specific pineapple plant which created a precise horticultural procedure. The first requirement necessary to produce the paltapina was a semi-tropical climate which played a key role in selecting the location of their Earth colonies. An area between the twentieth and thirtieth parallels provided them with a suitable climate to grow their cherished paltapina.

The paltapina was engineered to be the perfect diet for the Carinthians, being rich in proteins, carbohydrates, fiber, multi-vitamins, and Omega 3 fatty acids. Its darkish pink meat resembled lamb cooked medium rare with a texture similar to lobster meat. Their culinary experts had hundreds of ways to prepare the paltapina. Each changed the taste and texture in varying degrees, allowing the Carinthians to enjoy it as their primary food staple.

Smothering slabs of paltapina with mushrooms and onions resulted in something comparable to a thick cut of prime rib. They would also eat it stripped and sauced producing a pasta like dish. Or shredded and dressed to be eaten as a salad. As a snack, they would chunk and dry it, then eat it as a candy similar to salt water taffy. Frozen paltapina would be crushed and toped with sweet sauce and served as a desert.

The Carinthians also enjoyed other fruits; avocado, citrus, apple, peach, olives, and nuts. They maintained vineyards and loved wine. They developed vast plantations at each of their Earth locations, expanding them well beyond the needs of the colonies. Imported fruits, wines, and other fineries from Earth were sought after items on CarinaNova. These excesses provided nice profits when shipped back to CarinaNova.

The conflict free lifestyle, genealogy, and paltapina diet allowed the Carinthians to live an average age nearing two hundred years.

The Carinthians were monogamous, totally family oriented and very religious. In the typical home, the male provided the support and the female the environment. The female Carinthian spent much of her time keeping herself and her family preened. The physical structure of their homes was not large as their lifestyle had them at sporting events, salons, or recreational resorts much of their free time. Electronic power beamed to their homes enabled families to live in climate controlled comfort. Media also beamed to their homes kept them fully apprised of Carinthian events.

A typical commercial work schedule for the Carinthians was their equivalent of our five days a week with Saturday spent in family recreational activities. Sunday was set aside as their Sabbath. On that day they shut down all thoughts of vocation and sports to spend the time quietly reflecting on their relationship with their God and each other. Sports provided the Carinthians with the only conflict in their lives, which in reality was friendly rivalry.

Although relishing all forms of sports, the principal sport of all nations was a game called treos which resembled a mix of our soccer and basketball. Instead of a scoring net at each end of the court, scoring rings were suspended across the middle of the court. These rings varied in diameter, with the largest in the center.

Treos was played by two teams of seven to eleven players each, the object being for the teams to get the ball through the rings from their side of the court. A treos player could score three ways — by kicking, hitting or heading the ball through the rings. Each ring had a specific point value, with the lowest value being the large center ring. At each end of the arc of rings were the two smallest ones, attached to the outer walls of the court. These rings carried a point value over twelve times that of the large center ring. Players who could nail shots through these small rings were highly favored.

Treos was played very competitively by both male and female teams on the national level and extended all the way down to local neighborhood teams simply vying for bragging rights. The teams played in outdoor arenas and indoor climate controlled gymnasiums.

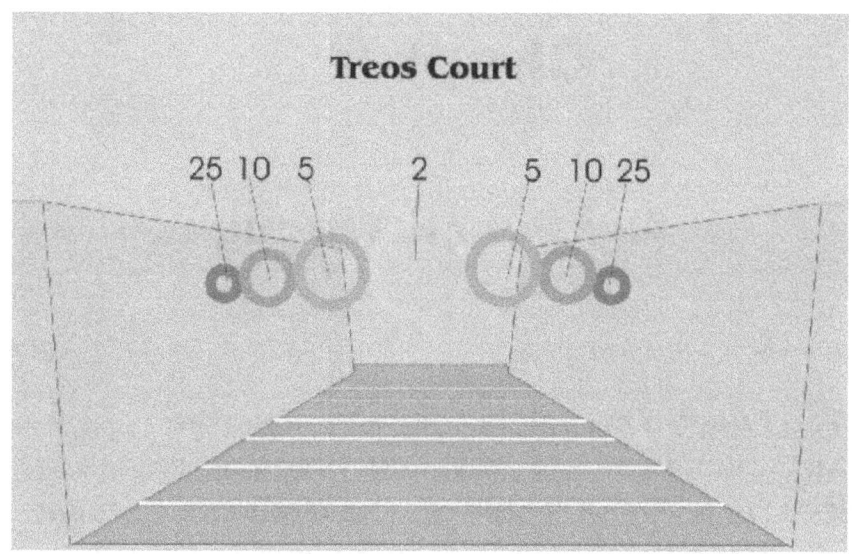

They enjoyed other outdoor sports as well. The males took pleasure in club sports such as fishing and hunting. The Carinthian colonists, not wishing to leave their sports behind, brought all elements of it with them to Earth.

Chapter 3

The Punch Through

The Punch Through is the technique the Carinthians used to travel very long distances in little time. This technique was available to them only when the Galactic Median was in a compressed state. Galactic Median was the Carinthian nomenclature for the dark space between all celestial elements.

Our scientists today refer to this as dark energy. This median is a gravity repulsive vacuum which comprises seventy percent of our universe. Dark energy is, in a way, the flux that holds our universe together and keeps mass from slamming into one another. You can envision it working similar to the way foam packing peanuts function to keep a china vase safe in a shipping carton.

The phenomenon called the *galactic spur warp,* a ten thousand year cycle where the tail of the Carina spur slowed, thus rolling the middle region of the Carina spur closer to the Orion spur.

This close proximity roll-in, or warp as the Carinthians called it, compressed the dark energy between the two spurs. During this period when the Galactic Median was compressed, the Carinthians had the capability of punching their airships through it. This close proximity period lasted for five thousand years.

The Carinthians developed a saucer shaped voyager, perfectly round and bulbous in the center. They outfitted these ships with powerful gravito-magnetic field generators which aggressively radiated artificial gravity beamed from the leading edge of their vehicle. Development of matter/anti matter annihilation reactors provided the most important breakthrough. These reactors produced the unlimited power needed to propel their ships at the velocity required to penetrate the median and produce a natural aversion which spit out their ships as if they were melon seeds. The Carinthians referred to this entire maneuver as the *punch through* or *punch*.

To perform the *punch through*, the missioneers would leave the CarinaNova atmosphere and accelerate at a full burn for fifty-seven days to a speed of near .76c (seventy-six percent of the speed of light). They needed this extreme velocity to drive them deep into the galactic median where their ship would be spit out the Orion side.

The actual punch took only minutes, not much longer than a tennis ball spends between the rollers in a serving machine. There was no opportunity to navigate during the *punch* process. The missioneers controlled their preferred heading reasonably well by selecting an entry attack angle to control the direction of their exit.

They built their ships with a profile identical from all aspects. This allowed some forgiveness for deviations in the pitch, roll, yaw and trim parameters. The most critical piece of navigating a punch was speed. Once the ship slammed deep enough into the median, it came out the other side. The ship's computers controlled all technical maneuvers of the punch through to avoid a catastrophic malfunction.

The missioneers experienced neither pain nor discomfort during the *punch through*. They traveled the punch in a special rig called the *Punch Restraint Apparatus* or *PRA.* They maintained a reclined position with their feet toward the bow of the ship, a precaution to keep the blood where it's suppose to be in the body during the punch.

As soon as the punch through was achieved, the navigators quickly calculated their current position and rebooted the course coordinates, possibly the most delicate piece of navigation on the entire voyage. The slightest error could send them years off course. At this point the navigators would need to make an aggressive equatorial right ascension using celestial sphere data shot off of CarinaNova. As soon as the navigators had their ship repositioned and locked to the corrected celestial heading, they sent a communiqué back to mission central that stated *We're on ER*th. This communiqué stuck as a reference for their destination planet. Whenever the Carinthians spoke about going to ERth they were not talking about Equatorial Right(ER), they were talking about Earth. Once established, the colonists would no longer allow their magnificent planet to be referenced with a synonym; it would be referred to as Earth.

After the missioneers had exited the *punch* and secured their correct heading, the Orion spur appeared as the only vision spanning the entire horizon in front of their ship. At that point the missioneers could discern our solar system. It would be twenty-eight days until they sensed themselves flying within the sun's light. Still decelerating from the momentum generated by the punch, they now had a visual on their destination – planet Earth.

In another six days they settled their voyager into a geostationary orbit and prepared smaller ships for the descent into Earth's atmosphere.

In time, the Carina and Orion spurs would roll back and separate, decompressing the dark energy. A *punch through* then would no longer be attainable. This would then close the door on intra-galactic travel for another five thousand years.

Chapter 4

Carinthian Air Power

In the early 7900's BC the Carinthians had the most punch worthy ship ever created, the massive heavy hauler. It was too large to be effectively operated in heavy atmosphere. Once built, they launched it into space where it would remain for its entire operating life. They maintained, refitted, resupplied, and refueled it in space. The size of this ship was mind-boggling even to the Carinthians at the time.

The ship sported six separate decks. It had quarters for eighteen thousand crew members and passengers.

The sixth deck, on top, held a very large storage facility with row after row of containers filled with consumer goods and gear.

Everyone traveling with the heavy hauler quartered on the fifth deck in close proximity to the commissaries, galleys and infirmaries providing the services they required.

The aft portion of the fourth deck belonged to JACOMM operations command center and quartered the JACOMM crews. Deck four's forward portion housed the ship's flight command and its personnel. Also in the forward areas of deck four were observation lounges affording the passengers sensational views of space.

Deck three, the hanger deck was capacious and could store two of today's largest aircraft carriers. The hanger deck contained thirty transporters and one hundred thirty JACOMM cutters. The heavy hauler had four launch and retrieval pads off this deck, one each from the aft port and starboard positions and one each from the forward port and starboard positions. These pads extended for each launch and retrieval operation. This extended pad system insured that in the event of a launch or retrieval accident, nothing would touch the outer skin of the heavy hauler. Any damage that could not be repaired in space would spell the end of its service life. The heavy hauler would no longer be capable of performing the punch through and would be scuttled in space.

The third deck housed the ship's reactors which were directly mounted on the blast ring circling the entire ship.

The ship's computers individually controlled the batteries of burn nozzles extending from the blast ring. Computers fully controlled the ship by varying the thrust and vector of the burn nozzles. On the aft portion of the blast ring, large blast nozzles propelled the ship forward at tremendous speeds.

Twelve matter/antimatter annihilation reactors powered the heavy hauler, each fueled to operate constantly at full capacity for over fifty years. These reactors were so mighty the heavy hauler could achieve punch through speed by burning only three reactors. Outfitting the heavy hauler with four times the power it needed guaranteed a wealth of redundancy. A power shortfall or failure would never keep the heavy hauler from being where the Carinthians needed it to be.

The first and second decks were large cargo holds. These decks would carry the one thousand metric tons of mined ore back to CarinaNova. The forward portion of the second deck contained the ship's teleportation facility. This facility both loaded and unloaded the ore onto or off the ship. In the loading process, the teleportation facility would receive the qubitized ore then direct it to the appropriate digital hold.

To unload the ore, the teleportation facility would boot the ore, then teleport it to a ground station where the ore would be detangled. This facility was a twenty-four seven operation the entire time the heavy hauler was on-station at either end.

Dedicated crews were assigned for each of the heavy hauler's areas of operations with no crew member ever having need to complain of being over worked. The separate crews consisted of the cruise crew, punch crew, on-station crew, launch and retrieval crew, logistics crew, maintenance crew, and the teleportation crew. The ship's supreme commander's job was insuring all his operation commanders were in top fly-worthy form. The operation commanders made sure their respective crews performed their individual functions flawlessly.

Maintenance and cruise personnel spent the most time on duty. These two crews rotated full on throughout the six to eight month missions.

Punch crews would come on call ten days prior to the punch to ready the ship and passengers.
They would also review all status lights to confirm the individual crews had their respective areas in punch readiness. This crew was also kept active for six days post punch.

Station crews reported two days prior to the heavy hauler settling in on its geostationary orbit. Once the ship was on-station, they took over the ship's operation. This tour lasted approximately two weeks on each end, but would be rigorous due to the intensity of the many ongoing operations being conducted.

Launch and retrieval crews probably had the cushiest jobs on the heavy hauler. They sat in nice quarters with a breathtaking view and directed the transporters and cutters on and off the ship. They were active two weeks prior and two weeks following the time the heavy hauler was on-station with one exception. JACOMM would occasionally light the *battle ready* array while in transit. If this happened, the crew needed to be ready to launch cutters instantly. The battle ready array would be lit if flight command had something on their trace radar that appeared abnormal. This happened more often than one might think. The Carinthians had no known extra-terrestrial foes but left absolutely nothing to chance.

To illustrate how vigilant they were, twenty of the one hundred fifty cutters on board were outfitted as interceptors.

These interceptors could quickly sweep a path five hundred million kilometers down range of the heavy hauler and could then deploy targeted drones. These drones were capable of traveling well above c and extended interdiction to three billion kilometers in front of the heavy hauler. Sounds ridiculous? Three billion kilometers represented only four hours of the heavy hauler's cruise. Assuming the anomaly on radar might be an aggressive enemy closing at the same speed or faster, the heavy hauler would potentially have less than an hour of survivability.

JACOMM didn't think in terms of kilometers, they used celestial-units referred to as CUs, a distance/duration equation. The Carinthians never had a foe, but at the same time they never assumed they were the only civilization with intra-galactic capabilities or, for that matter, intergalactic. The horrific part of this intense wariness was the fact that at those speeds any confrontation would be over before either party would have the opportunity to demonstrate non-hostile intentions. The Carinthians fully understood this, so battle ready always meant ready to kill.

From all appearances, the logistics crew had the least pleasant duty.

They physically moved freight between the sixth deck and the transporters during the loading and unloading process. Freight consisted of consumer goods and tools needed in the colonies, everything from crane parts to sugar.

Again, the teleportation crew were only active on-station. These were the nerds of their time, highly trained and uniquely skilled individuals. It took a high level of technical savvy to keep the teleportation equipment, a high powered super computer, operating proficiently.

Pilots of the transporters were only on call only while on-station, and flew just a few hours a day. Granted, flying entries and exits into and out of atmosphere required both nerves and skill and could certainly be life threatening and dangerous, but did not consume a lot of time. They spent the rest of the six to eight month tour playing treos, eating, reading, and lounging. Transporters flew twenty-four seven but each pilot only flew one mission per twenty-four hour period. They had great jobs.

On top of all this cross training, skill and redundancy of crew members, the heavy hauler's computers were programmed with a very powerful and constant *come home* algorithm.

This program constantly monitored the ship's environment. If this environment ever deteriorated into an unnatural operational configuration, the program would send a ship-wide alert announcing its intent to take command of the ship. If there wasn't an appropriate response to this alert, the program would seize control and configure an immediate return to CarinaNova. Once back on home station, mission central took over all operations.

Such precautions guaranteed the safety of the ship, its cargo, and crew in the event of life support systems failure or an attempt to commandeer the vessel. The heavy hauler, after generations of refinement, had evolved to the point of being almost impossible to disable or destroy.

Carinthians operated a sizable fleet of these heavy haulers. All heavy haulers and transporters were operated by private transportation conglomerates with their own crew and pilots. JACOMM maintained operations on each heavy hauler, including sole operation of the cutters.

The large transporter ships effectively slipped in and out of heavy atmosphere in order to transfer goods and personnel to and from the heavy hauler.

These heavy utility vehicles were manned by approximately twenty crew members, the number dependent on their assignment. They were outfitted with tripod extendable landing legs allowing them to set down almost anywhere.

The cutters were JACOMM's patrol ships and the only fighter type aircraft they allowed to be chartered. These little ships had extreme acceleration and maneuverability. They were not just pressurized, they had an inflatable membrane system that encompassed the crew and passengers. This membrane scrubbed off G-forces, allowing blooded personnel to ride on the cutter.

The cutter was outfitted with high powered directed wave noise emitters, processed light illuminators, mini-gig long range lasers, and the latch laser which was a short range charged laser that would strike its target and then latch on to it. This charged laser would latch onto its own heat, generated when it hit matter. All of these could be used as weapons, law enforcement tools, or just for domestic developmental support.

Compared to the transporters, the cutters were small ships with only three crew members. They had a passenger compartment capable of transporting ten individuals.

The cutter was also outfitted with a tripod landing system. It rarely set down in atmosphere, hovering instead. The cutter's various roles included patrolling, law enforcement, and assisting Carinthians in a multitude of domestic projects on CarinaNova as well as in the colonies. If necessary, the cutters were immeasurably lethal and functioned as the only volatile defensive system on the heavy hauler. Both the transporter and cutter were flying wings in atmosphere and razor edged rockets in space.

Chapter 5

Exploration of Earth

In 8068 BC, eighty years in advance of the first planned colonies, JACOMM had contracted for three heavy haulers to transport an exploratory mission to Earth in preparation for the colonization process. Each heavy hauler would carry thirty specially equipped transporters and another one hundred fifty cutters, to be used to explore Earth in order to update archival maps and charts. They would fly research missions gathering data which would be vital to the execution of the plan for the colonies.

Exploratory missioneers mapped the weather patterns and charted the expected frequencies of such patterns. They searched for suitable deposits of sought after minerals using infra-red thermo-graphic scanners, magnetometer recorders, and pan-frequency imaging radar devices. They took photo census of living plants and animals, and mapped their occurrence and proximity.

Exploratory missioneers spent months flying thousands of missions securing data. Simultaneously with this data retrieval, JACOMM assembled and categorized the information into specific tactical reports to be used by the Colonization Planning Commission.

One of the most troubling exploration discoveries by the missioneers - the infestation of aggressive and predatory animals. This infestation would be very cumbersome for the colonies.

Chapter 6

Extermination of Earth

In order to insure that all existing commitments to colonize Earth would be kept by all nations, JACOMM quickly formulated a solution to this newly discovered infestation. JACOMM pulled together a plan which they referred to as Omni-Lateral Extermination (OLE). This plan would be drafted using archival data covering a previous extermination project conducted by the ancestors. The time table for this plan was 8053 BC, sixty-five years prior to the first planned colony.

The plan called for precision matter/anti-matter air bursts which would radiate large areas of land mass with micro wave gamma rays. Gamma radiation would kill any flesh covered animal exposed to it. JACOMM's specialists had calculated each individual burst, detonated at an ASL (above mean sea level) of seventy-five hundred meters, would radiate a horizontal land radius of one thousand kilometers.

So the final draft determined there would need to be twenty-nine simultaneous bursts to adequately radiate Earth's entire land mass.

The plan specifically excluded the lower two-thirds of the continent we refer to as Africa from radiation as well as the Polar regions.

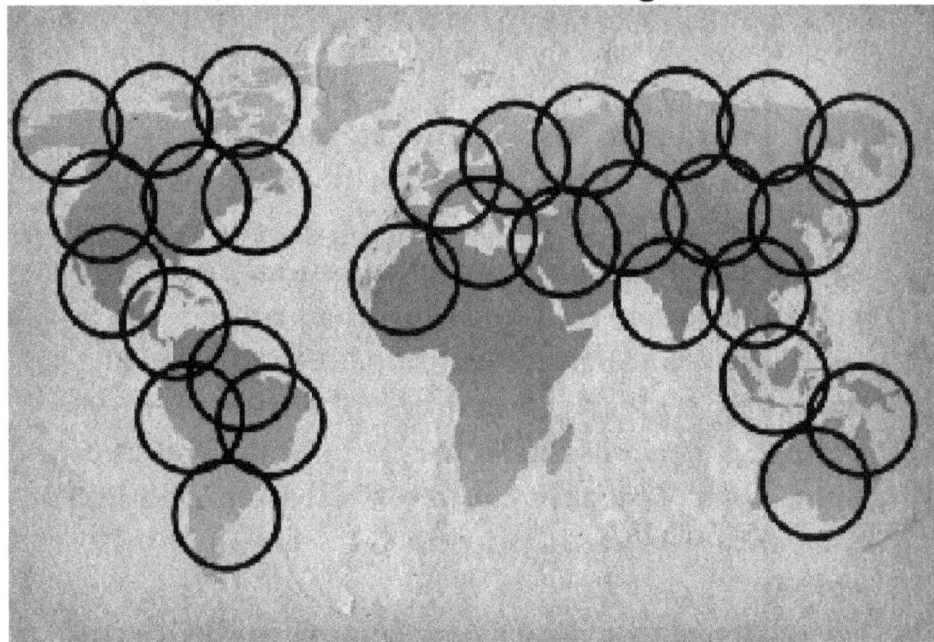

The plan would be carried out by seeding bomb laden drones, each programmed to hover on a specific coordinate indefinitely. JACOMM cutters were used to deliver and deploy these drones to their precise coordinate and altitude.

The drones were programmed to hover in place until receiving an electronic signal sent by JACOMM's command center located on the lead heavy hauler. Upon receipt of the signal, the drone would self-destruct setting off the chain reactive air burst. The air bursts were shaped so the bulk of the released energy would be directed toward Earth.

Immediately following the last drone placement, all cutters were directed to return to their respective heavy haulers. JACOMM would not permit aircraft in atmosphere during detonation. Several days elapsed following the placement of the final drone and confirmation that all cutters were fully battened in their hangers on the heavy haulers.

Before starting the countdown sequence, JACOMM requested that all engineers and specialists reconfirm their data to make sure no minuscule or obscure oversight had gone unnoticed.

They re-checked to insure the designated coverage area was being radiated. They double checked the anticipated climate change.
It had been factored there would be a four degree drop in the mean surface temperature of Earth post detonations due to lower carbon dioxide levels.

The directional detonation would also draw super cold temperatures from the stratosphere to the ground. JACOMM's projections said ground touching temperatures could reach as low as minus thirty Celsius. JACOMM wanted reconfirmation of data on the potential damage to vegetation and the data predicting the duration of the post detonation cataclysm. This data established the time table for the missioneer's return to Earth.

Countdown was not initiated until all data had been checked, rechecked and confirmed. The extensive count down sequence took two days to wrap to GO and was displayed in the upper left corner of every monitor on each heavy hauler and in the headquarters of OLE on CarinaNova. All group leaders experienced a combination of anticipation and anxiety.
What had they missed, miscalculated, or not seen coming? Everyone knew how crucial each calculation was for the plan to be usably successful. Even though every single participant in the operation knew and understood their duty, they still harbored a sinking feeling that the action could permanently eliminate Earth as a life supporting planet.

As the countdown drew near, every crew member and passenger on both heavy haulers were glued to the monitors.

Each monitor displayed a picture of Earth next to the countdown information. Exterior cams had been recoiled so the whole planet could be viewed. All portholes on the heavy haulers had punch shields in place to prevent direct observation. Heavy haulers, normally a beehive of activity, floated silently in an eerie calm, the only sound the distant muffled hum of the ship's reactors. Everyone witnessing this moment experienced a sense of guilt. The sight on their monitors had a definite impact on their senses. This beautiful planet bathed in sunlight appeared so heavenly peaceful, serene, and silent. They felt somewhat evil over what they were soon to do. The unrelenting countdown clicked off the time. Six more clicks and it would all be on.

When the monitors showed *GO*, the JACOMM commandant winced as he touched the orange broadcast button, sending a simultaneous electronic signal to all the hovering drones. When received, it set off a scuttle grenade and the drone self-destructed exposing the tiny capsule of antimatter to clouds of airborne microscopic matter particles.

An instantaneous clap of bright white light signaled the genesis of what would be a totally unstoppable chain reaction of celestial level revulsion which would continue until all antimatter had been annihilated. Rays of lethal gamma radiation flashed from beneath the cataclysmic explosion toward Earth, raining down on the stunned living beings that had impulsively looked up toward the sudden bright light. Before the Earth-shaking clap of thunder had reached them, they were dead.

The monitors on the heavy haulers showed the magnificent blue planet change instantly to an orange ball. Spikes of yellowish-white light visibly streaked out of the smoky canopy making it look as though even Earth's lightning was trying to escape this hell. In what seemed like forever, but in reality was only seven minutes, the bright orange glow began to fade. Within an hour the orange planet had turned to light foggy gray. One could still hear a pin fall on the heavy haulers. No one uttered a sound as they witnessed all life on Earth die. Even though Carinthians were very comfortable with their religion and believed fully they were carrying out the wishes of their god, they felt a strong sense of remorse.

On both heavy haulers, the public address systems which were seldom used now crackled with the JACOMM mission commander's broadcast announcing that Earth would not look normal again for the next eight years. Beyond that, Earth will have repaired and restored itself with the possible exception of a cooler climate.

Operation commanders of both heavy haulers now ordered their crews to prepare the ships for return to CarinaNova. The punch shields were now rolled off the portholes, affording everyone a direct look at the gray planet. The Carinthians, a philosophical people, did not like what they saw. All participants vowed to somehow get back to Earth to witness for themselves the planet's full recovery and hopefully alleviate some of their guilt. Very few of the OLE mission participants were aware that a large part of Africa had been left untouched. Neither were they aware that any living thing in caves, dens, boroughs or underwater would be spared from extinction.

Twenty cutters were launched to fly post detonation photographic missions, some to fly equatorial circumventions and others to fly polar circumventions.

The OLE mission commanders believed there wouldn't be much to see or photograph, that the Earth would be uniformly shrouded with the residual cloud cover even though there were areas left purposely unaffected. When the photographs were reviewed, the JACOMM mission commandant posted the notification "OLE Mission Successfully Complete".

Reactors on the heavy haulers were slowly brought to cruise power levels. The transporters, cutters and a multitude of other gear had been battened. Crews were positioned on station and the passengers had all retreated to their private compartments on the fifth deck for a period of quiet reflection and reverence. The time had arrived to commence the return trip to CarinaNova. As the heavy haulers rolled off their geostationary orbits and vectored the course toward their home planet, everyone that wished, had the opportunity to watch Earth slowly fall away. The mission and all that had occurred would now need to fade to memory.

Chapter 7

Colonization Commission

Back on CarinaNova, the Colonization Planning Commission had initiated a precise schedule. They forged ahead with full trust in JACOMM's extermination process fully assuming it would be successful and useable.

Those nations that had previously committed to colonization projects were now offered opportunities to submit their claims.

The right Climate, good soil, and fresh water were critical components for the development and maintenance of paltapina plantations a key priority in selecting the location of colonies.

While mining was certainly the principal purpose, the ability to grow sufficient levels of food remained the most important factor.

The nations of Egypturon and Cotazac, in that order, were the first to commit to colonies on Earth. Both were large, prosperous nations and each had extraterrestrial mining operations in place in the years leading up to 7988 BC. Both nations were very eager to relocate their mining operations to Earth.

As the initial claims were submitted, they were granted. Egypturon and Cotazac were issued permits to establish colonies on Earth effective with the first day of the year 7988 BC. Additional permits were issued to the other nations for the years beyond 7988 BC.

Egypturon and Cotazac put together the organizational plans, funds, and personnel to insure they were ready to jump from the blocks in early 7988 BC. JACOMM had agreed to provide support troops to assist the establishment and furtherance of all colonies. JACOMM would also provide full oversight and policing of all activity, both private and commercial, for the duration of the colonization of Earth.

The Colonization Planning Commission now had everything in place and Earth would soon, in a few decades, be the new home for many Carinthians.

Chapter 8

Special Breeding Program

As the long-range plans developed to colonize Earth, everyone involved faced what seemed to be an insurmountable hurdle - their plans would need a lot of manual labor support. The planners understood no Carinthian would choose to relocate from a cushy lifestyle on CarinaNova to work in the vineyards, bakeries, or mines on Earth. To colonize Earth in the aggressive manner they wished would require an absolute solution to this labor issue.

To resolve this problem, JACOMM pulled a *specialized breeding program* from the archives. This program was once used by their ancestors to breed work animals suitable for their needs. It was determined that such a specialized breeding program could be replicated on Earth to eventually provide the laborers required.

Using the archival data, JACOMM formulated a new breeding program and inserted in into the colonization plan. JACOMM's plan was to dispatch the breeding specialist forty-five years in advance of the first planned colony. This would give them time to have specimens ready to assist the initial colonies. The planning commission energetically endorsed the plan.

Now that the clock was running, JACOMM sanctioned and fully funded the project. They moved quickly to bring together a large team of their best biologists, headed by a group of experienced breeding specialists. In order to accomplish recruitment of the most capable professionals, JACOMM initiated a five year rotation in an attempt to present it as an adventure. The team of biologists would be supported by a large contingent of JACOMM troops who were also offered a five year rotation.

JACOMM perceived this program as a no-fail, non-ending venture, giving it unlimited support and funding. The program's success was integral to the Carinthians aggressive plan to colonize Earth. Knowing it would take thirty-five years to produce the first trained and educated work animal, the plan needed to be underway as soon as the first boots hit the ground.

The exploratory missioneers had located large communities of chimpanzees in central proximities of the continent now known as Africa. JACOMM considered these to be the perfect gen-stock.

Twenty-five years had passed since they effected the Omi-Lateral Extermination process. Recent surveillance missions provided proof of its success and indicated the lower two-thirds of Africa had indeed been left untouched. JACOMM knew Africa was teeming with wild animals, some very large and others dangerous predators. Assuring the biologists of their safety before deployment was of the upmost importance.

The plan called for the removal of all unwanted wild animals from a large controllable area of the rain forest near where the chimpanzees had been spotted. They would use high-frequency noise emitters to remove these animals. The emitters produced a sound so irritating the wild animals would flee to escape it. The emitters would then be strategically placed to keep this controlled forest secure from the unwanted animals so the biologists could do their work. The initial compound would be one hundred fifty kilometers long and one hundred kilometers wide, providing the ranging area the biologists needed for their project animals.

The deployment would initially need extensive well-equipped laboratories. It would also need a large contingent of troops to care for and assist the biologists. Everyone involved would need living quarters. These living accommodations and laboratories would be mobile, self-propelled units. Mobil units would allow the initial deployment to be flexible so the participants could expediently deal with any unforeseen weather, geographic, or tactical problems.

JACOMM selected an area in central Africa close large communities of chimpanzees, yet contained sufficient openings in the rain forest canopy for food production. The biologists were being pulled from a very comfortable lifestyle on CarinaNova. JACOMM wanted to assure those involved that they would want for nothing while serving their term on Earth.

The large contingent to Earth included culinary experts to guarantee the full detachment would be fed lavishly. JACOMM took every measure to ensure extreme comfort to all special breeding program participants and would keep a heavy hauler constantly on station, loaded with anything they might need.

The plan called for the biologists to commit to a five year rotation of service on Earth. This stipulation allowed JACOMM to recruit top professionals for the special breeding program who would keep it on schedule and guarantee success. All went well in the recruitment and the planning for deployment.

Chapter 9

Breeding Party Voyages To Earth

As previously mentioned, you and I are going to hop on board this flight and travel to Earth with the Breeding Party.

We have reservations to depart on this scheduled flight operated by the Celestial Logistics Limited conglomerate. All you need to do is stay with me. We will be traveling with several hundred biologists and special breeding experts along with eighteen hundred JACOMM support troops. The heavy hauler has accommodations for up to eight thousand passengers so we should have plenty of elbow room.

The prerequisites issued by Celestial Logistics Limited state we can bring only pre-approved items consisting of four flight suits, two sets of footwear, and our individual toiletries. We're each allowed to bring a computer or communication device, but nothing combustible.

The approved flight suit is one that can be cleaned and sanitized using compressed oxygen. There are no laundries on a heavy hauler. The approved footwear is a personally formed boot with soles and heels fabricated to be compatible with the floor surfaces on the heavy hauler. This is all to be packed in an approved flight case and pre-delivered to their facility.

On my travel day, I reported to the check in lounge at the Celestial Logistics Limited's operation facility. Using the automatic doors marked *Passenger Entrance,* I stepped inside their sprawling structure and proceeded immediately to the receiving desk stretching the full width of the building.

Approaching the first available representative, I was instructed to scan my confirmation seal. Then he snapped a short section of thin black material from a roll that looked like plastic tubing. He waved it across his monitor then fastened it around my left wrist like a bracelet.

He advised me the bracelet must be worn throughout the voyage, and the CL personnel would remove it once I was cleared for release on Earth.

He went on to say the bracelet contained a chip which allowed CL to monitor my whereabouts. It also would navigate me through the facility to the transporter. Once on the heavy hauler It would allow me to go anyplace on the heavy hauler where I had been given clearance. However, he cautioned, if I removed the bracelet after we were under way, I would be placed in restricted quarters for the duration of the voyage.

He instructed me to keep an eye on all the message boards. These boards provided all necessary information throughout the voyage. He then indicated the exit door to my left and told me to proceed in that direction.

As I walked toward the door, a rope cordoned everyone into single file and as I approached a message board lit up with my name instructing me to proceed to waiting area C.

I took a seat on the nicely upholstered benches and spent the waiting time studying my bracelet. It looked like a thin plastic tube with a barely visible embedded translucent chip. It felt as if I would spend less effort removing my hand than I would in trying to remove the bracelet.

Finally after a very anxious hour the message boards chimed and presented a readout—*Section C proceed to hatch #1 ramp for transfer to the launch pad*. Arriving at the ramp, I walked directly onto a monorail passenger coach which also carried freight to the transporter.

After a ten minute ride, the coach pulled up to the pad where my transporter sat in a launch posture. I now heard the whistle of the transporter's nozzles. The coach hatch slid open and I filed off, stepping directly onto a moving walkway which carried me upward toward the transporter's open cargo bay hatch. Once in, I fell into a queue heading to the entrance of the passenger compartment. Stepping through, a message board lit advising me of my assigned seat in section D.

As I proceeded along the aisle leading to section D, I walked past message boards at each aisle flashing my name and the words *Section D*. As I approached my section, the message boards listed my seat number as twenty-eight. As soon as I sat down, a message board on the back of the seat in front of me flashed a directive.

When the chime sounds, pull the restraint device to your chest. I mentally located the grab handle for the restraint device directly below the message board. With nothing to do but wait, I sat looking things over until finally the message board chimed, an announcement lit *launch will occur in twenty-two minutes.*

Ten minutes later the message changed, *launch procedures are now sequenced and launch will occur in twelve minutes.* My message board sounded a chime and flashed a brilliant blinking message *Pull the restraint device to your chest now.* I did and immediately felt it adjusting to my body until I was securely fastened to my seat.

The burn nozzles changed in tone, their whistle turning into a scream. My body felt very heavy. Had it really been twelve minutes? I caught myself wrapping my arms around the restraint device. It seemed as though my butt would surely break through the bottom of my seat. We had definitely launched. Having previously watched transporters launch, I knew the drill. Transporters performed a vertical launch straight up to approximately eight thousand kilometers ASL. It seemed to pause, then commenced a horizontal flight aspect.

I had just processed this thought when my heavy body suddenly went to weightless, no feeling whatsoever, my head pinned to the headrest on my seat and my body still in limbo. We now were in horizontal flight mode and I could tell by the sound of the nozzles this baby was cranking it. I tried to decide what to hang on to but was interrupted when the message board chimed. *We have now exited atmosphere and will be on board the voyager in forty-five minutes*. The muffled scream produced by the burn nozzles now seemed elevated in pitch. In exactly thirty minutes the message board lit. *We are on approach to 2420 BRAVO*. Ah, ha, I now knew the designation of the heavy hauler I had been assigned. I was going to Earth on 2420 BRAVO.

I soon felt muffled thumps beneath indicating we had locked on to the retrieval pad as confirmed by the new message now flashing. *We have boarded 2420 BRAVO. The debark tube is being attached and pressurized. Your restraint system will soon release, at which time you must immediately proceed to the exit hatch.*

As soon as my restraint system withdrew and positioned itself against the back of the seat in front of me, I stood up and looked for the exit hatch.

Falling in behind a forming line of other passengers, we moved single file and exited the transporter. The soft whistle of the transporter's burn nozzles told me they were once again at idle.

An exuberant sensation flushed through my body as I walked on board a heavy hauler for the first time. The lighting was bright, but somehow very soothing. The smell reminded me of a hotel lobby...a mosaic of food, flowers, and leather...although I saw none of this. The cool air refreshed while being easy to breathe. At the far end of this waiting area, I saw the other passengers filing through a hatch marked *Passenger Entrance*. I followed, and then the message board instructed me to proceed to chute two. As I walked toward the chute, a bell sounded and the door slid shut. The message board read *Full Weight*. I relaxed a few minutes until the chute door opened again. Several of us entered the chute and we were lifted two levels to deck five.

Deck five appeared idle, only the muffled sounds of boots walking the corridors. A number of message boards hung at eye level.
The first one informed me of my assignment to compartment fifty-four in community four.

I didn't know what a community was, but the direction signs on the corridor walls pointed me to my community. Once there, I noticed even numbered compartments on the left and odd numbers on the right.

My compartment was quite small, perhaps two and a half meters wide and two meters deep. I noted a high bunk mounted on the back wall and beneath it a couch-like piece of furniture which also was the Punch Restraint Apparatus (PRA). On the wall to my left was a rack for my flight case with a flight suit hanging clip above it. To my right a bathing area-toilet combination, no partition, not even a curtain. To bathe one rubbed your entire body with the furnished cleansing fluid, then stood beneath a large nozzle in the ceiling. Warm dry air quickly evaporated the cleansing fluid. I learned later this bathing method works wonderfully.

High on the wall to my right was a sizable message board(flat screen monitor).

Being curious, I flipped up the couch cushion exposing the PRA. Examining it, It looked like a gurney of sorts.
The instructions were written in English and explained how to secure myself in the PRA.

I recalled the seat restraints on the transporter and the weird sensation when they self-adjusted to precisely fit my body. A little shiver told me that one little malfunction of that much brute power working so close to my physical person could squash me like a June bug. Why do I think of stuff like that?

My whole cabin—toilet, PRA, bunk, walls—it all seemed to be made of the same material. It appeared to be a honeycombed titanium or similar bright metal with some type of embedded resin filler which apparently gave it great strength to weight characteristics.

My flight case finally arrived. I could now take a look around 2420 BRAVO. My message board showed a diagram of the ship's layout. It was laced with corridors and aisles. Even numbered corridors ran bow to stern while odd numbered ones ran port to starboard. The aisles had names rather than numbers.

I wanted to head in the general direction of the bow so I needed to locate an even numbered corridor. The posted signs showed the mall to my left, the infirmary to the right, and the galley straight ahead. My curiosity dictated that I check out the mall.

I found it to be nothing more than compartments, somewhat larger than mine but not by much. Each contained normal items and gear voyagers could purchase. Every little shop had a message board at the entrance that displayed your name when you passed through the hatch. My first thought said no way would anyone be able to shoplift. In reality, it allowed items to be purchased using the bracelet to bill them to the appropriate account. I wanted to see the galley next, so I followed the signs.

The first thing I noticed upon arrival was that all the fixtures looked as if they were assembled of the same honeycomb material. Most of the ship was apparently constructed of this. The galley appeared to be a large buffet, but didn't look large enough to serve eight thousand passengers. I later learned this galley only served the local communities. Most of the selections were of paltapina origins. They also offered a number of other fruits and nuts along with a few meats. Beverages were multiple labels of tea and coffee, water, and some fruit juices including paltapina juice. They also included a number of wine choices. Carinthians loved their wine.

This was fun, but I was dying to visit the lookout lounge.

I didn't see any directional signs showing me the way, so I approached a galley attendant and asked how to get there. He never looked up from his work as he told me to touch the question mark icon on a message board. Oh! I could use the message boards to receive information on demand, wow! I thanked him and went to the closest board where I did as instructed. Ten lines of options rolled up, the first one being *Ship Directions*.

With the route committed to memory, I started off at a brisk pace toward the lookout lounge. After what turned out to be a lengthy walk, I finally saw the dark portholes. As I hurried in that direction, I noticed the lit portholes to my right. I immediately thought *cockpit*, then saw the big banner identifying it as *Flight Command*.

Awesome! I tried to count the number of officers, but they were all moving around making it impossible to keep track. There must have been forty to fifty officers. Some sat at consoles looking into monitors, some stood at monitors, and others walked around working with a handheld device which seemed to fit their hand with a glove-like grip.

A few officers looked out the front portholes. There was one officer I assumed must be the captain, well, flight operations commander actually. He was definitely the most confident looking officer down there, walking around smiling, laughing, and patting others on the back. He also sported the most brilliant flight suit of all the officers. Watching all this buzz of activity mesmerized me. How long must it take to learn how to fly something like this?

I couldn't stand it any longer. I had never seen space before and needed to take a look. I moved forward to the lookout portholes. There she was. CarinaNova, sitting out there in all her splendor, the most beautiful sight in our view. She actually didn't look that far away. It was difficult for me to comprehend that just a few hours ago I had been walking around on her. Wow! What a truly stunning view. I saw both moons and what looked like a transporter flying toward CarinaNova. I wandered to myself if it was the transporter which we had just flown on. I perched on one of the observation stools and simply shut down for a while and took in the marvelous sight.

I returned to my compartment when I received a message advising that we would be rolling off of station in two hours and needed to ready the PRA for use when the chime sounded. After preparing it, I decided to hit my bunk until I received further instructions.

The chime startled me awake. The message board instructed all passengers and crew members to be positioned in their PRA at this time. 2420 BRAVO would roll off station in forty minutes. I jumped down from my bunk and positioned myself on the Punch Restraint Device following the instructions. I was ready. Why wasn't anything happening? I was almost afraid to move a muscle. My message board chimed again—*we would roll in ten minutes*. I heard hissing sounds and felt the side tabs adjusting to my body.
My head protector adjusted so tenderly it reminded me of a mother's touch. This thing definitely had me tethered down yet nothing was happening. I waited. Could this be an E-ticket thing? The concept amused me to the point where I couldn't stop the grin. It seemed as if I'd been there forever, although actually less than thirty minutes.

Then I heard the hissing sound start up again. Had something gone wrong? A mechanical malfunction? My restraint device retreated, first my head protector then my side tabs. The message board chimed, announcing that we were underway and all personnel were free to move about the ship. That was it? We had already rolled off station? I hadn't felt a thing. Bummer!

After walking around and talking with some of the other passengers, I finally convinced myself we were indeed full on underway to Earth. Amazingly on this heavy hauler, one didn't experience any sense of movement or sounds that would indicate we were rocketing through space. Nothing.

The next several days were spent acquainting myself with my surroundings, eating a lot, and spending a great deal of time in the lookout lounge. Unfortunately, there wasn't much to see except darkness. I could see distant stars and planets, whatever they were, but they just sat out there. I had expected to see streaks of light flashing past us, after all we were flying near 76c. I thought things would be zinging around out there. Not so.

With so much free time on our hands we filled the days by playing treos, eating paltapina, watching some treos, visiting the lookout lounge, playing some more treos, drinking wine and tea and coffee, then watching some more treos. The missioneers had their own teams and some kind of league with scheduled games, very competitive games.

At this point we had been flying for forty-eight days and the message boards had been keeping us apprised of the upcoming punch through sequence. Everyone in the galley talked over breakfast, lunch, and dinner about the punch through. It was the big thing anticipated by everyone. To be honest, as a result of all the talk I had grown a tad anxious over this looming event. I told myself I had no reason to worry. After all, if things went catastrophically wrong, I would never know it.

Six days passed with the ship in punch posture status. A punch ops officer came to my compartment to discuss the procedure with me, mostly just apprising me of what to expect and when. He reassured me the punch would have a duration of only hours, but I would need to be in readiness several hours in advance of the occurrence. As I would be spending over four hours locked in the PRA, I should plan and prepare accordingly. I got the drift.

I picked up one little fact from visiting with everyone. There was no exact moment the punch initiated. Apparently they flew the ship at maximum velocity, knifing her deep enough into the median to where the power of the universe took over and **BLAMO**! We then went where the power of the universe took us. There never seemed to be a timetable for this.

The punch through readiness countdown was well underway. The message board told us we had six hours before the get ready chime sounded. The six hours ground to four, then two hours, and finally the chime sounded. A message constantly flashed on the boards saying all passengers and crew members must now be in their PRA. I had been cautioned repeatedly by the punch ops officer, that if I didn't properly restrain myself I had to assume the consequences. There would be no one checking on me and there was no holding pattern on the punch through sequence.

I prudently positioned myself in the PRA and the device adequately pinned me inside my cocoon. I had been there for over an hour, a very long hour. I had been forewarned about this monotony.

My message board continued to flash *must be restrained* which had grown quite annoying. After an hour and a half, I imagined I'd developed bed sores. DING DING. A new message announced 2420 BRAVO had locked on punch sequence and punch would commence within the next sixty minutes. Anxiety grabbed hold of me. Thoughts filled my mind, telling me how insignificant my life was at this point.

    Whoa! I couldn't breathe, couldn't move. We must be punching! I panicked. Could I keep myself under control? I fought to keep myself from losing it! Then I heard the ventilation system kick in and a sense of relief swept over me along with the cool air. I could breathe again. The ship had adjusted the internal pressure, my ears normalized. The ship's vibrations resonated to me. This couldn't be good. I rolled my gaze around my compartment to make sure nothing was coming apart. Why did I waste my energy worrying? If the ship came apart, I wouldn't be alive long enough to know it. Damn, anxiety had a mean grip on me. I sensed the ship groaning, WHAT WAS THAT? I should have done a better job of mentally preparing myself. For the first time in the last two months, I felt this monster of a vehicle buffeting! 2420 BRAVO was buffeting! I hoped the ship could handle it.

I tried to feel my feet. Were they on the stops? Was my head still being held by the head protector? I didn't know. It felt as if my blood pressure had sky-rocketed. I wondered if my bracelet was sending my vitals to anyone. Or for that matter, if anyone cared. All the med techs were in their PRA's. I felt as if I was going to pass out. I couldn't keep my eyes open. Oh my God. What was happening?

    I woke to the hissing and clacking sound of my restraint device relaxing. I slowly lifted my head and glanced around my compartment. All appeared normal, everything intact! I checked my message board. Blank. Then a chime sounded and I locked my gaze on the message. *We have acquired the Orion spur and all personnel are free to move about the ship*. Could it be true? I sprang from the PRA and threw my arms up in victory. I had just ridden out a punch! NOTHING TO IT!

    Call me crazy, but as soon as I gathered my thoughts I wanted to see the Orion spur. I burst from my compartment and headed toward chute four. I finally reached the lookout lounge, gasping for air as I stepped inside.
I suppressed a slight grin as I looked around the lounge. Apparently I wasn't the only crazy on the ship.

The lounge bulged with onlookers. No way was I going to get a first hand look that afternoon. I barely got a glimpse through the crowd, but managed to pick out the one most thrilling feature, the one everyone seemed so excited about. Earth's solar system. It appeared as a distant lantern, a lone flare out there in the blackness.

I turned to leave, making my way to the porthole with the view into flight command. Why was I not amazed?
Less than an hour off the punch and everything looked perfectly normal down there. Same smiles, same rhythm. It all looked the same. I would have thought they would be running around adjusting levers and switches while yelling and receiving orders, waving arms and hands. But no, none of that. Order and calm projected a fully under-control environment. They all looked as though they would never permit anything to go wrong.

The next thirty days seemed to drag, unlike the first sixty. Perhaps the post punch syndrome coupled with the excitement of getting to Earth. I found a news bulletin posted on the message boards. I loved reading those posts. It said we would be penetrating the sun's heliopause in two days. At that time 2420 BRAVO would finally have the light of our destination's sun shining on its hull.

Those two days passed quickly. From our vantage point inside the sun's heliopause, the scene from the lookout lounge had improved immensely. I could now see planet Earth. From today's position, Earth looked like a little bright blue gem, lying in a black sea of tranquility.
I saw a back drop of what appeared to be smaller planets behind Earth.
I was sure they were not smaller, just much farther away. Those planets appeared to have been partially and unsuspectingly ferreted out of their dark enclaves by the sun's relentless search light.

Hey! A very large rock just streaked by on our port flank. Yikes! An asteroid field? I knew the ship had powerful radars which continually tweaked our heading, but could they pick up all the little asteroids and meteors? I knew we were *gassing it* out through here. I'm sure a football size chunk could take us out? Damn it, why do I do this to myself? I had never heard of a heavy hauler breaking up flames. We would be ok. As I left the lounge, I glanced down into flight command, the same casual scene. Why do I worry?

I read today's news post about our approaching entry into our first outer Earthly orbit at 1100 hours tomorrow.

We have been decelerating for the last six days and would use two orbits to scrub off the speed we had to lose so we could settle into our station. The post went on to say *we would be on station within forty-eight hours.*

I received a chimed message that my community would debark on day four. Again quoting from the news posts, *no one would be leaving the ship the first day on station.* On day two, only critical personnel would deploy to Earth. The remaining passenger list would transfer days three through five, using a predetermined transfer schedule messaged to each individual.

Four days had passed with me still on station, but today at 1600 hours community four was scheduled to transfer. I had my breakfast and took my last look at Earth from the lounge. What a sight, sitting on station about thirty-six thousand kilometers ASL, and Earth appeared like a stunning gem on a dark satin cloth. It looked a lot like CarinaNova from station but definitely a brighter blue. Perhaps because of the unpopulated status Earth enjoyed or possibly Earth had a greater ocean to land mass ratio. Whatever the reason, it looked perfect. I was anxious to get down there. I read so much about Earth's fresh air, perfect weather, and total quiet.

I found it difficult to sit in my compartment waiting for the message board to give me my marching orders, but I didn't have any choice in the matter.

I kept looking down the hall to make sure I hadn't missed my call while everyone else was busy transferring. Time had dragged on since lunch. I tried to bring up information on the message board, but when I checked the transfer schedule it continued to show everything on schedule.

My message board finally chimed and flashed a notation telling community four to report to the transfer deck for transport to Earth. I shot out of my compartment, flight case in hand.

The walk to chute eleven seemed to take forever. Once there, I fell in line behind a number of other anxious looking passengers. It took twenty minutes to get down to the transfer deck. It had the same exciting, refreshing feel as the day I first walked onto it. We waited for instructions to proceed through the debark tube and onto the transporter. A member of the logistics crew gathered our flight cases and stacked them on a shuttle cart over to the side.

A chime sounded and message boards throughout the transfer deck instructed us to board the transporter. As I did, the message board advised I had seat thirty-eight in section C.

As I sat down, I felt weak from anticipation. Thirty minutes elapsed as all passengers located their seats.

Finally the message board chimed announcing, *We will launch in eleven minutes*. The restraint system gently pushed me back into my seat and I was ready to go. The message board flashed that launch would occur in six minutes. While mentally counting off the six minutes, I recalled the aggressive launch from CarinaNova. This time I was prepared for it. With a firm grip on the restraint system, I waited for the launch. One could hear the burn nozzles raging. I was ready this time. The message board chime broke my concentration. *We have departed 2420 BRAVO.*

What happened? I didn't feel anything. I settled my arms and looked around at the other passengers. It appeared to be just another flight to them. The message board lit *We will be setting down on JACOMM's forward base, 42-2 ALFA. We will debark on Earth at 1840.*

Chapter 10

Deployment of the Biologists

When the first biologists deployed to Earth in the year 8033 BC, they positioned themselves in central Africa. Their initial site required proximity to large communities of chimpanzees along with enough space and a suitable climate to grow their own food, most importantly the paltapina.

They located their first makeshift headquarters in a forest of mature Baobab trees with magnificent overhanging canopies and massive copper colored trunks. Just to stroll around the base of one of these palatial columns could take a full minute. As they stood beneath the canopy, thousands of sun beams surrounded them, pouring onto the emerald carpet of lush floating ferns and waving grasses. Birds provided a mind soothing serenade. A myriad of fresh fragrances assaulted their senses. This was as close to a *Garden of the Gods* as they had seen. The biologists felt as if they had found a piece of heaven.

They discovered an interstate type system of trails in the forest. These trails had been created by the large elephant herds that roamed central Africa. These herds were so large that watching them parade by in single file took a better part of the day.

Their initial laboratories were the self-propelled modular units brought in from the heavy haulers on transporter ships. The sizeable, fully articulated self-contained units came outfitted with walking wheels so they could traverse anywhere a trail existed through the forest.

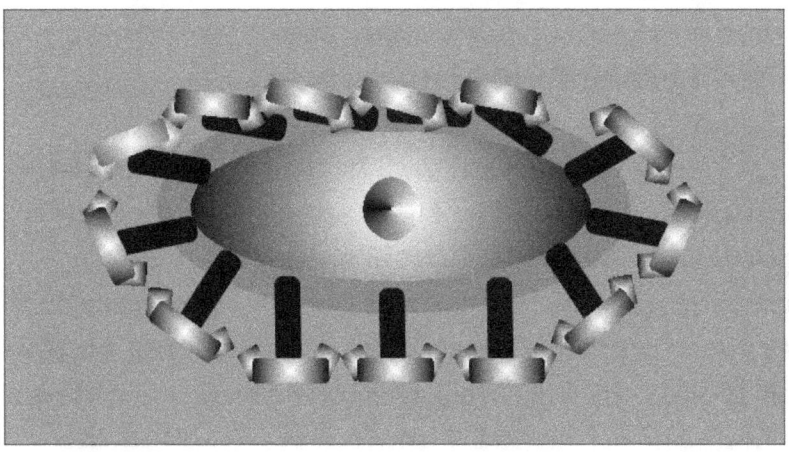

The very first project for the biologists was to round up the female chimpanzees required to get their mandated breeding operations underway. The biologists were assisted by three JACOMM cutters brought in for the purpose of flushing the chimpanzees from the trees and immobilizing them. The roundup would be a highly coordinated effort between the cutters and a ground crew and would kick off as soon as the target community had been selected. The chimp communities always nested in trees surrounding an opening in the forest and it would be in this opening where the capture would occur. The entire roundup organization was ready to mobilize immediately after sundown when the chimps had retired to their freshly made nests.

Three cutters moved in first, hovering in a semi-circle just above the canopy. On a given signal, they activated their emitters and illuminators. The emitter sound, a reverberating roar, continually elevated until it became so loud that it literally vibrated the bellies of the chimps. At the same time the illuminators flooded the forest with a bright orange light permeated with bright yellow flashes. This array simulated a raging fire, frightening to both man and beast.

Immediately following the activation of the illuminators and emitters, the once naturally peaceful evening forest erupted in a clamor.

The frightened chimps shrieked, screeched, and cried as they poured from their nests. They hurriedly swung from limb to limb in an attempt to get to the ground anyway they could. It had the appearance of someone tipping over a box of ants. Once on the floor of the forest, the chimpanzees fled in the direction that would seem to take them away from the bellow and the fire.

Due to the position of the cutters, their direction of escape led them right across the opening. As the frightened chimps scampered onto the fern carpeted ground, the cutters moved in and illuminated them with a dielectric resonance beam. This beam penetrated the chimpanzee and immediately slowed its body rhythms to the point where the chimp quickly fell into a sleep-like trance, leaving it with no apparent concerns. All shock and fear had waned.

Once the cutters had the chimps immobilized, the ground crew moved in wearing full body suits and helmets to protect them from the dielectric beam. Without the protective covering, the beam would immobilize them as it had the chimps. The ground crew selected healthy females ten to twelve years of age along with a few dominate males as semen donors.

Once a female chimpanzee was selected and tranquilized, they moved her into the mobile laboratory and checked her for an existing embryo. If they found an embryo, it would be aborted to make her ready for artificial insemination. The process consisted of extracting semen from the males, then washing a sperm with a predominant Carinthian gene. The altered sperm would be used to fertilize an egg removed from the female. Once fertilized, the egg would be placed into the uterus in a position that would allow the biologist to confirm conception within twenty-four hours.

Once inseminated, they placed the female chimpanzee in a holding birth to observe her until they could confirm conception. Once conception had been confirmed, a tracking and monitoring chip would be implanted and she was taken into the controlled forest along with twenty to thirty other freshly inseminated females. This sizeable controlled forest, a zone one hundred and fifty kilometers by one hundred kilometers, had been cleared of all other animals. The noise emitters kept unwanted animals out of the controlled area and kept the treated chimpanzees in.

As the freshly worked chimps were released into the controlled area, they were positioned around the trunks of the baobabs out of sight of each other.

Next to each recovering female, the biologists piled a meal of figs and dates. She awoke from the anesthesia famished, then immediately devoured the newly discovered meal. As she overcame her anesthesia and her hunger disappeared, she noticed the other treated chimps in the vicinity. Within a few hours they had bonded, roaming, ranging, and foraging together totally unaware of the traumatic change that had just happened to them.

This ongoing artificial insemination process continued in an assembly line fashion until the biologists had inseminated thousands of female chimpanzees. Caretakers electronically monitored each of the females twenty-four hours a day. They kept constant track of her location and general health of both her and her embryo. This monitoring went on for nine months and as the birth hour grew close, the biologists moved in to be near.

They knew the offspring would have such a strong Carinthian genome that it would be abandoned by the mother chimpanzee and if left alone would live only hours after being abandoned. They needed to be very near so they could retrieve the newborn within minutes of the birth and move it to the laboratory.

Once in the lab they fed it intravenously for several months until it could eat on its own. The female having just given birth would soon be brought to the laboratory to be re-inseminated.

When preparing the semen, the Carinthians engineered the gender attempting to produce predominantly female offspring. This engineering effort worked ninety-seven percent of the time which left three percent of the offspring as males. The males were a very unfortunate by-product of the breeding process. The Carinthian religion would not allow them to be euthanized, now that they carried Carinthian DNA, so once these males were five years old, they were released back to the rain forest knowing these male chimps would live out their lives without mates and would struggle to feed themselves each and every day.

The female offspring, on the other hand, were immaculately cared for and nurtured in every way while kept under constant surveillance. Once the female offspring reached puberty, at about six years, they were ready to be inseminated for the second tier of the breeding process. The second tier went through the exact same process as the first tier.

The biologists kept up this breeding process through four tiers. On the fourth tier, the semen had been re-engineered to produce a more natural fifty percent males and fifty percent females offspring. These fourth tier offspring would now sire the animal the biologists had set out to produce.

The fifth tier produced magnificent beautiful animals who would eventually be mated with each other rather than being artificially inseminated. They had now evolved with strong Carinthian-like physical features and a Carinthian like brain, meaning it had a large frontal cortex. The biologists referred to this strain as the *fifties*, meaning fifth tier, and now were no longer releasing them to the forest.

As the initial stages of the breeding program played out, virtually every biologist who had agreed to the deployment became captivated by the utopian surroundings.

They found themselves living and working within what they considered a *sacred scenic garden*, laced with beautiful blue lagoons, teeming with magnificent birds and animals. The sights, sounds, and fragrances coupled with the nearly perfect year around climate, mesmerized them. All but a few applied for extended deployments, claiming they didn't want to leave work undone. They also applied to have their families brought to Earth. Perhaps the more accurate explanation would be that they didn't want to leave the paradise they had discovered. Most of the supporting troops also applied for extensions and to have their families brought to them.

Once the breeding program participants solidified their extended deployment, they forged ahead of schedule with the construction of permanent homes and facilities. The commandant of the breeding program had summoned master builders, into Central Africa. The biologists issued contracts to construct laboratories, temples, stadiums, salons, and homes. All were to be constructed using only the finest stone and wood, a luxury long lost on CarinaNova.

To JACOMM's delight, the special breeding program was now being remarkably executed by a skilled fraternity of dedicated and motivated members.

Many of them lived out their lives in Central Africa.

Chapter 11

People

JACOMM, an organization not tolerant of failure, had the pressure turned all the way up on the breeding institution. Everyone involved with this breeding program were kept on a very aggressive and highly prioritized schedule. JACOMM had vital need for a usable work animal of adequate intelligence, but also educated and trained. These work animals needed to be capable of providing productive support for the soon to be established colonies. Two nations were scheduled to establish their Earth colonies and each expected twenty-five hundred of these animals.

The breeding program had initially been quite successful in producing good quality animals and had succeeded in delivering a specimen that fully met or exceeded all original assumptions and expectations.
With the breeding phase well under control, the program transitioned into an aggressive curriculum of training and educating the newly produced animals.

Once in training, the trainers no longer referred to the work animal as fifties. They were now referred to as *people*.

Wasting no time, the trainers had two year olds viewing educational videos for the better part of every day. The educational videos were scaled down versions of the videos used in the home schooling educational progression on CarinaNova. At the age of three, the trainers began adding personal hygiene to the curriculum. The new people were taught to hygienically care for themselves, their quarters, and their surroundings. In this period of their training, these youngsters had hardly a moment to themselves.

They knew no fear, because nothing ever threatened them. They knew no greed because they constantly had everything they needed. Any temper eruptions were quickly penalized using exclusion tactics and the withholding of treats. By four, the youngsters had an adequate vocabulary using the language of the nation's colony where they would be assigned. Their writing lessons largely learning to use keyboards and touch screens. The Carinthians did little actual hand writing themselves. All their written correspondence was done with electronic devices. Writing paper just did not exist.

By age five, the trainers had these new young people fully regimented. They were sharp, clean, happy new people. The males were kept from the females. There would be no mating until after they were transitioned into the colonies. They were educated about what to expect when finding a mate and once found, how they would be expected to treat that mate. They were tantalized, using the opposite sex in order to develop healthy mating desires. The trainers took them all the way through the procreation process and how to care for their young. Natural skills pertaining to procreation and caring for young certainly should have been built into the breeding process, but the trainers left no opportunity for failure in this area.

Simultaneous to the educating and training of the young people, the breeding specialists continued to produce large numbers of new infants. The entire program matured into a systematic progression, with highly skilled and motivated specialists at every position. To say the breeding institution had turned into a *people factory* would not necessarily be a misnomer.

While this almost hectic program of churning out people surged forward with enthusiastic brilliance, another issue needed urgent resolution.

The new people would require a diet high in protein. The Carinthians planned to produce large numbers of people and soon they would be self-propagating and all would need adequate food supplies. At the same time, the Carinthians preferred to not feed them the much cherished paltapina. Any and all of the paltapina production would be consumed by the Carinthians or exported.

It had only been twenty-five years since the Carinthians had virtually wiped most of Earth clean of all living animals. The issue of an ongoing adequate supply of provisions for the new people needed to be resolved. While the bulk of the breeding specialists were busy producing people, a small group was assigned to develop domesticated feedstock animals, principally sheep and cattle. Feedstock animals were bred up, using the same process previously used in producing the work animals.
Wild Mouflon sheep were captured and genetically refined using genes brought in from CarinaNova. Domesticated cattle were produced from Cape buffalo, in the same manner. This small group of breeding specialists soon had flocks of domestic sheep and herds of domestic cattle grazing in nearby pastures. These feed stock animals would move in unison to the colonies with the people.

Meanwhile, the young people, now at age five, were transitioning into their vocational training curriculums. The males were training out in the plantations, vineyards, orchards and fields. Some were being trained to care for the newly developed sheep and cattle. Others were being trained in landscaping and as gardeners. The original purpose of the plan to develop people was to provide coverage on aforementioned vocations for the colonists.

The females entered totally different training regimens. They were trained in food preparation, laundering, infant care, and a number of other domestic duties. Again, these were areas where the colonists would need the support of these people.

All the young people soon had full-fledged assignments. They were taught the importance of reliability, responsibility, and productivity. The young people were easily molded into their new assignments, work and responsibility being the only thing they knew. Their newly assigned tasks felt very good, leaving them proud of their accomplishments without the need for any type of play or entertainment. They were never mistreated, overworked or martially punished. The Carinthians coddled these people, rewarding their advancements. They embraced these young people as precious.

The new beautiful people had been developed using prominent genes drawn from the gene pools of the individual nations committed to take them. As a result, the people had uniquely different physical characteristics. The fifties had a very strong resemblance to the Carinthians they would soon serve.

With so much at stake and so many Carinthians assuming success, it was paramount for the biologists to lock onto a very aggressive production schedule. They were Carinthians, however, and appropriated plenty of recreational opportunities. Most Carinthians fully enjoyed outdoor sports like fishing and hunting. These were expensive club sports on CarinaNova, but ample and unlimited for those deployed to Central Africa.

Newly established treos leagues played with the biologists opposing the JACOMM troops. Treos teams grew to be enormously competitive and the games became the key entertainment for the breeding institution participants.

Throughout the breeding process, the biologists had systematically washed the tiered sperm with a very prominent Carinthian gene. This prominent gene progressively lightened the complexion of the work animal.

By the time the Carinthians had produced the fifth tier, it emerged as an animal with a very light olive complexion. The biologists anticipated this change would progressively evolve into lighter complexions as these animals further propagated, due to the ongoing dominance of the Carinthian gene.

One of the most skilled breeding specialists on tour in central Africa found himself wanting for another challenge. As a hobby, he took it upon himself to attempt to develop what he referred to as an *exotic breed of people*. As an experiment, he washed a sperm lifted from a fifth tier male with a gene from a second tier male. He then fertilized a fifth tier female egg and then used this egg to inseminate a fifth tier female. The result, to his amazement, was a beautiful bronze skinned animal with a brilliant brain. His hobby exploded, now being joined by a number of equally enthusiastic biologists, and within a few years they produced a full black complexioned, large brained animal. The biologists called these exotics *nitori*, a name which made reference to their splendid, glowing, elegant bodies.

The excitement grew over the nitori, considered as thoroughbred animals to be used solely for enjoyment and entertainment rather than work.

The nitori were not committed to the colonization projects and remained in central Africa. The biologists and trainers taught the nitori to play Carinthian games, hunt, and fish. They also instructed them in playing musical and percussion instruments, singing, and dancing.

As these thoroughbreds matured, the Carinthians became enamored with them. They were brilliantly complexioned with keen athletic physiques—magnificent animals. The nitori were mated and kept as families in eloquent quarters, adorned in brilliant garments designed to flatter their toned bodies. They were fed well, using a diet high in paltapina to further enhance their brilliant complexions and physiques. The trainers instructed them in how to play treos, forming both male and female teams. The Carinthians would spend hours watching the nitori play treos. They enjoyed being entertained by the music and dancing performances of the nitori. The biologists nurtured both the black and the bronze strains of nitori. They proudly announced and promoted their existence to their fellow Carinthians on CarinaNova.

****

In Volume 2 you will spend time with the people, getting to know and enjoy them all. You will spend time with the nitori and will find them as pleasurable and captivating as the biologists did. The new people had never witnessed evil or malice of any sort. You will be intrigued with their approach to life. You will transition with them to the colonies where they will explore their new surroundings. You will experience the pristine environment enveloping the newly formed colonies on this paradise called Earth.

www.ingramcontent.com/pod-product-compliance
Lightning Source LLC
Chambersburg PA
CBHW031455040426
42444CB00007B/1110